WITHDRAWN

Thanksgiving

by Natalie M. Rosinsky

Content Adviser: Dr. Alexa Sandmann, Professor of Literacy,
The University of Toledo; Member, National Council for the Social Studies

Reading Adviser: Dr. Linda D. Labbo, Department of Reading Education,
College of Education, The University of Georgia

Let's See Library
Compass Point Books
Minneapolis, Minnesota

Compass Point Books
3722 West 50th Street, #115
Minneapolis, MN 55410

Visit Compass Point Books on the Internet at *www.compasspointbooks.com* or e-mail your
request to *custserv@compasspointbooks.com*

Cover: Eastern wild turkey

Photographs ©: Richard Day/Daybreak Imagery, cover; Photo Network/Michael W. Thomas, 4;
Mark E. Gibson/The Image Finders, 6; Bettmann/Corbis, 8; Giraudon/Art Resource, N.Y., 10;
Maslowski/Visuals Unlimited, 12; Photo Network/Esbin-Anderson, 14; Michael Philip Manheim/The
Image Finders, 16; Unicorn Stock Photos/A. Ramey, 18; AFP/Corbis, 20; John Cross/The Free Press, 24.

Editor: Catherine Neitge
Photo Researcher: Svetlana Zhurkina
Photo Selector: Catherine Neitge
Designer: Melissa Voda

Library of Congress Cataloging-in-Publication Data
Rosinsky, Natalie M. (Natalie Myra)
    Thanksgiving / by Natalie M. Rosinsky; reading adviser, Linda D. Labbo.
       p. cm.— (Let's see library)
Includes bibliographical references and index.
    ISBN 0-7565-0391-4 (hardcover)
    1. Thanksgiving Day—Juvenile literature. [1. Thanksgiving Day. 2. Holidays.] I. Title. II. Series.
    GT4975 .R67 2002
    394.2649—dc21   2002003183

Table of Contents

What Is Thanksgiving?

Think about a feast, a family gathering, and late November. If you add up these clues, you will know what time it is. It's time for Thanksgiving!

Each year, Americans observe this national holiday. Thanksgiving Day is the fourth Thursday in November. Schools, businesses, and government offices are closed. Many families eat big dinners of special **harvest** foods. They may thank God for the good things in their lives. Sometimes, people enjoy parades and sports on this day.

Thanksgiving **celebrates** a good harvest. It also celebrates the very beginning of our country.

◄ *Turkey is the main dish at a Thanksgiving feast.*

What Led to the First Thanksgiving?

Long ago, many people celebrated their good harvests. This **custom** continued through the centuries. People also thanked their gods after they had lived through hard times. The **Pilgrims** who came to America in 1620 knew both customs.

The Pilgrims had sailed bravely across the ocean in the *Mayflower*. They wanted their own community. They wanted to pray to God in their own way. Their trip was hard and full of danger. Their new life was hard and full of danger, too.

In 1621, they had their first harvest. Half the Pilgrims had lived. They had reasons to give thanks.

◄ *A replica of the* **Mayflower** *is docked in Plymouth, Massachusetts.*

What Happened at the First Thanksgiving?

About fifty English people lived in that new community called Plymouth. That autumn, they were joined by ninety of their Indian neighbors. The **Wampanoag** people had helped the Pilgrims. They showed them how to grow a kind of corn called maize.

There were three days of feasting, races, and games. This kind of celebration was also a Wampanoag custom. People ate turkey, fish, and maize. They may have had cranberries and pumpkin, too. The only pies at that feast were meat pies!

◀ *The Wampanoag and Pilgrims celebrated the first Thanksgiving.*

How Did It Become a National Holiday?

Thanksgivings for good harvests continued, but the story of the Pilgrims' celebration was lost until 1820. Then, a book written by one of the Pilgrims was found. Until 1863, states had their own Thanksgivings. Communities celebrated for different reasons and at different times.

A famous writer named Sarah Hale wanted a national holiday. She thought this would honor the Pilgrims. She also thought it would strengthen our country. President Abraham Lincoln believed her. In 1863, he made the last Thursday in November our country's Thanksgiving Day.

◄ *This nineteenth century print by Currier & Ives shows the Pilgrims landing at Plymouth Rock.*

Why Is the Turkey a Symbol of Thanksgiving?

The turkey is native to North America. The Wampanoag taught the Pilgrims how to hunt this wild bird. It was likely part of their Thanksgiving feast. Turkey was also enjoyed at other times.

Turkey was part of the harvest the Pilgrims celebrated. The turkey has become the main **symbol** of Thanksgiving. It is often eaten then. Pictures of turkeys are also used as Thanksgiving decorations.

◄ *Wild turkeys walk through the snow.*

What Are Other Thanksgiving Symbols?

The *Mayflower* is one of our country's most famous ships. It is a symbol of Thanksgiving. The Pilgrims may have landed at Plymouth Rock. This rock is also a symbol.

Pictures of how the Pilgrims and Wampanoag looked are other symbols. However, Pilgrims did not usually wear tall, dark hats. Often, they wore bright colors.

Harvest foods like pumpkins and corn are Thanksgiving symbols. One very old symbol is part of Thanksgiving. It is a horn of plenty that over-flows with fruits and vegetables. It is a **cornucopia.**

◀ *Harvest foods are symbols of Thanksgiving.*

How Has Thanksgiving Changed?

Thanksgiving has been celebrated on different days. In 1939, the president moved it from the *last* Thursday in November to the *third* Thursday. He wanted people to shop more between Thanksgiving and Christmas! This change was not popular. In 1941, Congress moved Thanksgiving to the *fourth* Thursday, where it remains.

Another change is how people see the Wampanoag. In 1972, they were honored at our nation's capital. Still, many Wampanoag feel sad and angry on Thanksgiving. They believe the Pilgrims and later colonists hurt their way of life.

◄ *A woman shows how the Wampanoag lived in the past.*

How Is It Observed in the United States?

Parades were part of harvest celebrations. Together, people would bring in the last crops. People today may walk in or watch Thanksgiving parades. This usually happens in big cities.

Enjoying a feast with family and friends is another custom. Giving food to people in need is a custom, too. After a good harvest, farmers did this. Turkey, pumpkin pie, cranberries, and corn are Thanksgiving favorites.

Some families pray together. They give thanks to God. Playing games and watching sports are other customs. Football is very popular!

◄ Huge balloons highlight the annual Macy's Thanksgiving Day parade in New York City.

How Is It Observed Around the World?

Canada has its own Thanksgiving Day. In this country to the north of the United States, crops are harvested earlier. Canada's Thanksgiving is the second Monday in October. Family feasts and parades are also Thanksgiving customs here.

Germany, Holland, Sweden, and Switzerland have a different Thanksgiving. The people in those countries celebrate on November 11, Saint Martin's Day. This is when birds and animals have grown big enough to eat.

In India, some people honor a harvest goddess. They celebrate for three days.

◄ *Geese hurry across the road near Hamburg, Germany. The goose is a symbol of St. Martin and a favorite food on St. Martin's Day.*

Glossary

celebrate—to enjoy and honor something

cornucopia—a horn that is always full of food. The first cornucopia is in stories about the gods of ancient Greece.

custom—thing regularly done by a group of people

harvest—gathering in of a crop when it is ripe

Pilgrims—the people who traveled to America in the 1620s to start their own community

symbol—something that represents something else

Wampanoag—the name of the group of Indians who were the Pilgrims' neighbors

Did You Know?

- Pilgrims used spoons, knives, and hands to eat. They did not use forks.

- Sarah Hale wrote many poems. Her most famous poem is "Mary Had a Little Lamb."

- No one is sure how the turkey got its name. It may have been mistaken for a peacock from India.